7 Pillars

of

Wisdom

Wisdom House Publishing
Knoxville, TN 37950

Wisdom hath builded her house, she hath hewn out her seven pillars.

                    Proverbs 9:1

7 PILLARS

OF

WISDOM

by
Hallerin Hilton Hill

Wisdom House books may be purchased for educational, business, or sales promotional use. For information please write: Special Markets Department, Wisdom House Publishing, PO Box 51661 Knoxville, Tennessee, 37950.

FIRST EDITION, 2000

Library of Congress Cataloging-in-Publication Data
Hill, Hallerin Hilton
      7 Pillars Of Wisdom/Hallerin Hilton Hill
      ISBN 0-9676778-0-7
      1. Self-help. 1. Title

Jacket design by Andrea Truan
Book design & typesetting by Karol Cooper

1 2 3 4 5 6 7 8 9 10 · 00

To Nedra, Hallerin II & Halle

You gave me love
You made me new
You gave me everything
When you gave me you

Acknowledgments

I remember meeting Alex Haley once and hearing him say, "If you ever see a turtle sitting on a fence post, he had help." This book didn't just happen. **I had help**.

Special thanks to Rabbi Howard Simon, Dr. Max Robinson, John Peck, and my friends at Johnson Bible College for helping me with the research. My friend Criswell Freeman was a godsend: Thanks for teaching me the ropes. Thanks to Alan Ross for all his help on the edit, and to Karol Cooper for the typesetting and lay-out. And to my friends at Morris Creative Group — Chuck Morris, Todd Greene and Andrea Truan — thanks for making the art-work sparkle. Thanks to John Wright for teaching me courage.

I have been inspired by many people in my life. I thank God for my parents, Dr. Franklin S. Hill II & Mrs. Lucille E. Hill. Words can't convey what you mean to me. My brothers, Franklin, Byron and Roland — it's great to have you in my corner. My sister, Terry Harris — thank you for being my special friend all these years. My brother-in-law Michael Harris — you're a hero to me. To my friend Shelbert Gaines — thank you for being such an awesome friend, you're the best. Special thanks to my in-laws Roscoe & Annette Bolden, to Dedra & Tim and their family, and to Brian and his family. And I can't forget my Grace In Motion brothers — Kenny, Chris, & Devin — you keep on blessing me with your gifts.

I know there are others that I might have missed, but know in my heart that I am grateful to all of you. Thanks for helping this turtle get up on the fence post.

HHH

Table of Contents

Introduction

It was absolute pandemonium. My pulse pounded in my chest like a thousand tribal drums as I stopped my car and jumped out. The sounds of terror filled the air. Bloodcurdling screams were coming from every direction — a chorus of chaos in surround sound. The night sky was filled with foggy black smoke that rushed up from the piles of death and debris all around me. Fires were everywhere; the heat was unbelievable. I could hear sirens in the distance. I choked on smoke as I ran across the highway, stepping in pools of fresh blood along the way. Everywhere I looked there was blood — warm blood splattered on cold metal. There were at least ten planes down, and more were circling above me in total confusion. The roar of jet engines was deafening. Hands reached up in agony as I stepped over bodies and fragments of bodies. There was no time to stop to help. I had to get to the control tower to see what was going on. I hit the stairs, taking them two at a time. Breathless, I arrived at the tower only to find that no one was there. I was alone and I had no idea what to do. The radios were squelching with controlled panic as the pilots trapped in this foggy night called for instructions. The phone rang and I picked it up, hoping it was someone who could help.

"Hi, this is Carl from MasterCard. You've just been approved for a new Titanium card with a $200,000 limit!" said a used-car-salesman voice on the other end of the phone. I slammed down the phone and looked around the room at all the computer and radar screens. I was clueless. When the phone rang again, I snatched it up and cried, "I need some help and I need it now!"

"Well, sir, this is your lucky day," said a perfectly manicured voice on the other end. "This is J.B. from Acme Motion Pictures.

"We want to make a movie about you and this tragedy. We're gonna make you a star. Your name will be up in lights. You're gonna be famous, kid."

Who could talk about money and fame at a time like this? What I needed more than anything was the skill to know what to do. "I don't need fame or money, I need to know what to do in this control tower!" I screamed, slamming down the phone. Then I heard a voice — warm, confident, deep and restful. Against the backdrop of disaster, it resonated hope.

"Son, I've been around here for 35 years."

I looked up to see an old janitor. His hands wrapped around his broom the same way Perlman holds his Stratavarius. He said, "I got here as fast as I could. I know this place like the back of my hand." He looked at the bank of screens carefully, analyzed the situation, then handed me the mike. "Just push the buttons I tell you to push and say the things I tell you to say and everything will be alright," he said with a reassuring smile. "My name is Sam. My friends call me Wisdom. The boss sent me to help you."

And so ended my dream. What a picture! Have you ever found yourself in the control tower of your life, clueless as to what to do? I sure have.

This book is about wisdom. This book is about taking control of your life and living more powerfully and skillfully. So with this book I want to do two things: (1) Define wisdom and (2) Help you make wisdom the foundation of your thinking. I want you to erect seven pillars of thought that will revolutionize your life.

Much of what I write about here is gleaned from the collected Proverbs of King Solomon. There's a lot of good stuff there. King Solomon found himself in Israel's control tower at the age of 12. There were a little less than a million people in the kingdom when he took over. What does a 12-year-old know about leading a nation, even if he is a prince? Solomon knew that he didn't need more "stuff." He didn't need more "toys." He needed wisdom. Solomon needed to know how to lead. He needed to know what to do in the control tower to manage his great empire. What he needed was skill. So Solomon asked God for wisdom.

When I was a boy my mother read the story of Solomon to me. From the first time I heard the story, wisdom has been my constant craving. If you picked up this book, I can make one assumption right off the bat: You, too, hunger for wisdom. You long to know how to live skillfully. This book contains tools to make your life richer and more abundant. Applied wisdom has changed my life. It will change yours. I love wisdom. Wisdom is sweet! Now it's your turn to taste it.

Craving Wisdom

I want you to fall in love with wisdom. I want you to crave it. I want wisdom to become a part of your DNA. So I am writing to make wisdom so attractive to you that you fall in love with it.

Every month, I read through the Book of Proverbs — 31 chapters in all, averaging one chapter a day. Reading the Proverbs has opened my eyes. I live more skillfully than I did before I started learning from the Proverbs. It will work for you too.

Now, don't think this book is only a religious book. Remember these truths have been tested in the crucible of history. They work, whether you believe in God or not, in much the same way gravity works whether you acknowledge Sir Isaac Newton or not.

Why Pillars?

"Wisdom hath builded her house, she hath hewn out seven pillars." Proverbs 9:1

Scholars have long debated the symbolic meaning of the seven pillars. In writing this book, I had the pleasure of spending some time with Dr. Max Robinson, head of the College of Architecture and Design at the University of Tennessee. He stated that pillars were the primary support elements of much of early architecture. The pillars held up the buildings. Back then, pillars were very large. Some were 20-30 feet in circumference and 80-100 feet tall. Because of their size, they could offer a lot of support and were stable. You could build upon them with confidence. The heft of the pillars gave man a sense that his world was not going to fall down on him.

Pillars were also used to make a statement about the importance of the building in society. Pillars were used in constructing temples — where the most important contact in the universe was to take place — man's interaction with God. Pillars were used in building courthouses and financial centers as well as to erect palaces.

Pillars have three distinctive elements: the base, the shaft, and the capital. Some philosophers speculate that pillars were a representation of man; the base being his feet, the shaft being his body, and the capital symbolic of his hands lifted up to God as he tries to hold up his world.

For our lives to be powerful we must build with the right kinds of pillars. The materials from which we build those pillars will determine how well we "hold up" in this fantastic journey we call Life. Our thoughts are our pillars, and the way we think is the hammer and chisel that sculpts our lives.

Pillars are a wonderful metaphor. Strong pillars make strong structures. So it is with your thinking. As wisdom is the foundation or support system that undergirds your thinking, your life will be built on wisdom. A life built upon wisdom is strong and powerful. It is full of joy, wealth and peace.

Here, then, are the Seven Pillars of Wisdom — seven pillars of thought that will help you create and sustain a life full of joy, peace and wealth.

1. **Fear God**
2. **Fall in Love with Wisdom**
3. **Joyfully Submit to Discipline**
4. **Walk with the Wise**
5. **Master Your Money**
6. **Lead from the Inside Out**
7. **Lend Yourself to the Poor**

These are the kinds of mental pillars that you can build on with confidence. These pillars are the foundation of wisdom. These pillars make your life better.

Before we take a closer look at each of the pillars let me give you my definition of wisdom.

"Wisdom is highly developed skill and insight applied at the right time to produce the right results for all the right reasons."

We'll take a closer look at the definition of wisdom in chapter two. Are you ready? Here are 7 Pillars Of Wisdom.

*The fear of the Lord is the
beginning of wisdom.*

Proverbs 1:7

Pillar 1

Fear God

Fear God. God must be in first position in your life. Walking in the fear of the Lord produces confidence and courage to face life's challenges. How much better would your life be if you put God first?

Personally, I hate the word fear. My initial response to the word is negative because I hate the feeling of being afraid, of being dominated. As a little boy, I hated going to school because I dreaded confrontation with the bullies in my class. As we pulled up to the school, I'd see them on the schoolyard and my heart would race. I looked for ways to cross the schoolyard undetected. I hated the fear I was feeling at least as much as the fear I felt for the bullies. That's not the kind of fear I'm talking about here. In this context "fear" means respect. To "fear" God is to stand in reverential awe.

For example, if you were a struggling basketball player and Michael Jordan came to your house for a personal coaching session to help improve your shooting, how attentive would you be to his instruction? You'd hang on his every word and would follow his instructions to the letter. Why? One word — **respect** — because you know that he knows what he's talking about. You know that the wisdom he's sharing with you is the same wisdom he has used to become a basketball legend. You stand in awe of his talent and skill, and that awe makes you more focused and teachable. That is what it means to fear God. It is to put God at the head of your life and see to it that He stays there.

In Proverbs 1:7, which states, "The fear of the Lord is the beginning of wisdom," the word *beginning* is tricky. One gets the impression that wisdom merely starts with God. But, in the Hebrew, the word "beginning" has a much broader meaning. "Beginning," in this context, also means foundation and/or best part. It is true that wisdom starts with God, but it is also true that God is the *foundation* of wisdom. God is the beginning, middle and end of wisdom. That principle is central to growing in wisdom. You must see God as awesome and be constantly blown away by His majesty. You must marvel at His power and wisdom. When you see God that way, you are drawn into the most sincere form of flattery — imitation. You start to crave wisdom and skill and order in your world. You long to know on a deeper level this God of limitless wisdom. Simply stated, to fear God is to reverence, respect and receive Him.

The great theologian, John Peck, told me in an interview that, "God is to wisdom as the alphabet is to books." You can never read or write a book without first having an intimate knowledge of the alphabet. So true wisdom begins when you put God first. It begins with respect. Fearing God has a lot to do with how you think about God. The wise man is the man who reboots his thinking and learns to think about God in the right way.

God is big. By comparison you're not. The right-thinking man sees God as big. I was looking at a satellite photo of earth recently, and I couldn't find myself in the photo. I'm too small. God made the earth. God authored all her systems and cycles. And this is just one of many planets and solar systems. Knowing that leaves me awestruck. Knowing that helps me catch a glimpse of just how big and powerful God is.

When you stand in awe of God, power and wisdom flow into your life. How, you say? God has infinite wisdom, infinite skill, and that wisdom and skill were used to create the world and the systems and cycles that sustain and maintain it. Respect for God positions you to learn from God. You learn more from people you respect and are in awe of because they have your undivided attention. When God has your attention He can share His wisdom with you.

The Five Benefits of Fearing God

Now that we've defined fear, let's address how we can expect our lives to change as we walk in the fear of God.

There are five major benefits that emerge by putting God first in our lives and making a reverential awe of God a pillar of thought for us.

- **Peace and Happiness**
- **A Fountain of Life**
- **Confidence**
- **Riches**
- **Honor**

When God has our attention, when we trust His infinite wisdom, when we look to be led by that wisdom, we are *shaped* by that wisdom. To fear God is to reverence that wisdom. We are empowered when we establish a personal, working relationship with the author of all wisdom. In that personal relationship we are given access to His infinite wisdom. The first noticeable effect is a greater sense of **peace and happiness**. This is due to the fact that we now know we are no longer limited in life. We know that the author of all wisdom is allied with us, ready to help us succeed. That relieves anxiety.

Anxiety often comes from not knowing what to do. Moreover, people don't know who to turn to for the answers. So they worry. Bobby McFerrin's "Don't Worry, Be Happy" is a great song, but it doesn't work for many people. It does, however, work for the person walking in the fear of the Lord, because it is logical to release worry and be happy if you've got direct access to all the answers. So as you cultivate a deep-seated reverence for God, expect to be happier. See God as big enough to handle anything that comes up in your life and watch in amazement as you start to grow in infinite wisdom.

The second benefit of fearing God is a **fountain of life**. One cannot stand in the presence of a limitless God without being enthused and energized. When a tree takes in light it takes in energy. The light becomes life. The same is true for man. When he opens himself to God he receives life. One who has reshaped his thinking so that God is properly reverenced experiences a constant spiritual refueling. Respect causes you to pay careful attention. The more I watch highlight films of Michael Jordan, the more I am both amazed and inspired. When you see God's wisdom at work it will inspire you. It will charge you with life.

For example, I love music. I love to see exceptionally gifted musicians do their thing. I remember attending a very powerful concert once. The musicians were playing their instruments with overwhelming perfection and mastery. As I feasted on their musical excellence I became inspired. The experience energized me, and I left the concert not only moved, but with a desire to develop a similar level of excellence and mastery in the things that I do.

So it is with those who fear God.

See His majesty. As you revel in His wisdom and are energized by it, something even more magical happens: You start to crave the excellence that is the embodiment of God, and it fills you with life. That reverential awe for God becomes a life-giving inspirational force; definite electricity charges your life when you walk in the fear of the Lord. It pushes you toward the things that bless you and away from the things that harm you. With reverential awe for God, we are moved to emulate the attributes of a limitless God, moved to do the things that sustain and improve our existence because the very nature of creation is regenerative.

Another benefit of fearing God is **confidence**. I know what you're thinking. Those two words — fear and confidence — would not seem to go together, but in this context they do.

Imagine for a moment that I told you that you had one hour to create a computer using only things in your kitchen. What if I added that if you couldn't get it done, I'd kill you. How confident would you be that you could accomplish your task? I would be a nervous wreck.

But what if I told you that if you picked up the phone on the wall in the kitchen you would be linked directly to former Microsoft CEO Bill Gates, the king of the computer world, and that he had been instructed to use all of his resources — his wealth, wisdom, planes, helicopters, 40 thousand employees — to meet any request you made. How confident would you be then?

I'd say very confident, and rightly so. You would be confident not because you had power, but rather because you have access to the power you need. You gain a strong confidence from watching God's wisdom at work day in and day out.

And that wisdom working day after day brings yet another benefit — **riches**.

Caution! The word "riches" evokes images of swimming pools and movie stars. You can almost hear Robin Leach oozing out tales of champagne dreams and caviar wishes. Please understand that riches of the spirit are much more durable than hardware. When we walk in the fear of God, we find our greatest riches in the peace and wisdom that saturate us from beholding His excellence. As evil is driven from our lives and replaced with excellence, as our confidence grows in His limitless power, as we become more energized and enthused, we discover a richness of spirit that is sweet. We find peace of mind. And peace of mind is true wealth.

I was watching an interview with Jean-Claude van Damme, the kickboxing action-movie superstar. The interviewer asked him what he wanted most in life. His reply? "To be at peace with myself." The same is true for the super successful hip-hop and rap producer, Sean "Puffy" Combs, better known as "Puff Daddy." In an interview in *Essence* magazine, he confided that even after making more than 50 million dollars in one year what he longed for most was peace of mind.

You're rich when you have peace. There is room for material wealth. And as we emulate the excellence of a limitless God, we draw material wealth into our lives. A person at peace with himself, a person full of godly confidence, a person full of life and enthusiasm, is a magnet for wealth.

The final benefit of fear is **honor**.

What I love about standing in awe of God is that it shapes us. We cannot worship at the feet of unlimited wisdom and power without being transformed. We find honor in the association.

For instance, in the music industry a lot of name-dropping goes on — name-dropping that works on some levels because of the transfer of honor that occurs from association. In my own case, I was fortunate enough to co-write a song that appeared in the movie "The Preacher's Wife," starring Whitney Houston. A degree of honor was conferred upon me because of her incredible talent. The same thing happens from our association with a God that is full of infinite wisdom. As people see us change and grow in wisdom, we are inevitably showered with honor. So walk in the fear of the Lord, and expect peace and happiness, a fountain of life, confidence, riches, and honor.

Walking in the Fear of God

In order to benefit from this new and powerful way of thinking, new habits must be installed. First, as we've seen, walking in the fear of the Lord is the practice of reverencing God, meditating on His limitless power, His majesty, His wisdom.

Walking in the fear of the Lord is also about the elimination of evil. The presence of evil can have a crippling, devastating impact on your life. There are four particular traits of evil that, left unchecked, can ultimately stifle your pursuit of wisdom. These traits are:

- **Pride**
- **Arrogance**
- **The Evil Way**
- **An Evil Tongue**

Pride

Pride limits growth. Proud people can't grow because they can't be taught. They know it all. If they can't be taught, then they can't grow and mature. It's as simple as that.

The proud person is also easily manipulated by people or situations that don't allow them to be in total control. All you have to do to reduce that kind of person to a useless pile of reactionary response is challenge them and their pride. From that point forward, they work in defense of their pride, not in making the best decisions or moving forward. These people end up spinning their wheels.

Power and wisdom come from releasing pride. Releasing pride also clicks with the notion that we don't know it all. We don't have to know it all. That's God's job. Our job is to know who knows.

Letting go of pride also puts us in a position to look for the best solution to every challenge in life, rather than just the solution that best protects our pride. Part of walking in the fear of the Lord is realizing the destructive nature of pride, then conscientiously turning away from it.

Along with the release of pride the person actively walking in the fear of God will abandon arrogance. Arrogance is defined as overbearing pride. Now there is such a thing as "good" pride: To be proud of hard work and positive accomplishments is fine. Arrogance, however, is obnoxious. It is pride at its worst made manifest in a person's behavior.

The proud person has himself at the center of his universe. The wise person has God (infinite wisdom) at the center of his universe. Remember, you can be no bigger than your center.

Arrogance

Pride isolates us from God. It severs our internal connection with God and His wisdom. Arrogance drives people away, which further isolates us. If you think about it, that's the way many cults are able to brainwash their followers — by isolating them from growth, from everything that would compete with the cult's message and its ability to control. Isolation weakens self-control and places a person more firmly in the control of others. Pride is **internally** destructive, arrogance is **externally** destructive. The end result is that you feel isolated and weak.

I don't know about you, but I can't handle being around arrogant people. Arrogance tends to drive me away. In the same way, arrogance drives God away. In order to be truly arrogant, you have to believe that you're "IT." If you believe that, then you cannot be taught. You cannot receive wisdom.

Arrogance, then, is the outward manifestation of inner pride — pride that separates us from God, and arrogance that separates us from people and opportunities that offer potential growth.

The Evil Way

Just as the person who walks in the fear of God must daily relinquish pride and arrogance, they must also depart from the evil way. Proverbs 6:16-19 clearly states that God hates "a proud look, a lying tongue, hands that shed innocent blood, a heart that deviseth wicked imaginations, feet that are quick in running to evil, a false witness that spreads lies, and a man who stirs up dissention among brothers." So if you want to walk in the fear of the Lord there must be a willingness to have your whole body — your eyes, your tongue, your hands, your heart, even your feet — void of evil. The fear of the Lord demands a certain amount of inner purity. When evil has not been eliminated from our lives, we waste so much time and energy dealing with its fallout. Truth must be a sacred standard. Evil must be eradicated. Pride and arrogance are twin evils. They paralyze the soul. They stifle growth. They smother wisdom.

In our win-at-all-costs society, there are many people who don't care who they have to crush in order to get what they want. Your life should be free of that kind of contempt for your fellow man. Be certain to use your intellect for **good**. It's incredible how intensely focused evil people can be in the pursuit of their pleasures. How many movies have you seen where a killer has planned the perfect murder, or a bank robber has planned the perfect heist? What a waste of intelligence! What would happen if everyone used their minds to pursue true wisdom and goodness? The wise man guards his heart and his intellect to be sure that he doesn't waste time thinking up evil schemes.

The same holds true for the things we rush to be a part of. If it's our desire to walk in the fear of the Lord and to grow in wisdom, we must not run toward evil. Every step taken toward evil is a step away from God. Every step away from God is a step away from wisdom. The wise man sees evil coming and hides from it. Walking in the fear of God means putting an end to those activities that create strife.There are those who enjoy the power that comes from having created tension, but that person will never know true wisdom.

An Evil Tongue
Your tongue can get you in a whole lot of trouble. The tongue is connected to the soul, so when your soul is full of filth, your tongue is filthy. If you follow that logic, then it only makes sense that as you eliminate evil from your inner world, you will eliminate evil from your outer world. Your tongue and the way you speak announce to the world what's important to you and the direction of your thinking. What you talk about says a lot about how you think. If your mouth is full of wise words, if you have learned to speak when it is important and useful, and to refrain from speaking when it is not, you will be well regarded. On the other hand, an evil tongue easily identifies you as a person void of wisdom. It also shows a profound lack of respect for your infinite God.

Spreading negative information about others is poison. It makes you feel terrible about yourself. When you are in the presence of someone you've gossiped about you feel like a traitor. It's a dirty feeling. That feeling zaps your power. Gossip breeds paranoia. The fallout from a wagging tongue is also time-consuming because once started, gossip must then be managed. Wisdom cannot flourish in the mind of the gossipy person.

To walk in the fear of the Lord you must remind yourself every moment of every day of the majesty of God, and you must depart from evil. Understanding that as you walk with God, the source of unlimited wisdom, you will grow in wisdom. You don't need the distraction of evil. Evil demands attention and keeps your focus blurred. And the attention that you give to evil is attention that you cannot give to God or the wisdom He wants to share with you. Wisdom begins with fearing God. Not in being afraid of God, but in having so much respect for God that you become teachable. Wisdom means respecting God enough to imitate Him. Growing in wisdom starts with respecting God.

How do you apply the fear of God in your life?

Order your life so that it radiates respect for God and eliminates the evil that you find.

Wisdom is the principal thing; therefore get wisdom; and with all thy getting get understanding.

Proverbs 4:7

Pillar 2

Fall in Love
With Wisdom

Fall in love with wisdom. Crave skill and excellence. Yearn for it. Make wisdom a part of who you are, what you do and how you think. It is the gateway to all you can desire. How much more effective would you be if you craved excellence in everything you do?

Love is the most powerful force in the universe. It cannot be conquered.

They met in the cafeteria line at college. From the very first moment he saw her he was smitten. Before they knew it they were dating. Every time he was in her presence his hands got cold and sweaty. His heart raced. He was working two jobs and going to college, so finding time for a relationship wasn't easy. But he found the time. Somehow he wrung another hour out of each day. He was in love and love found a way. Love gave him energy. Love gave him strength. Love made him focused. His love for her restructured his priorities so that he could give her the time and love she needed to make the relationship work. Love caused him to make sacrifices. The neat thing was, he never felt like he was making sacrifices. He would go to classes all day, work most of the evening but when the time came to visit with her he was bursting with energy. He should have been totally exhausted, but love lifted him. You see, I was that young man, and Love lifted **me**.

It is with that in mind that I move forward to introduce you to the second of the seven pillars — falling in love with wisdom. I use the word "love" because I'm not merely trying to help you understand wisdom; I am not merely trying to give you a beautiful vision of wisdom. No, I want you to do more than merely notice wisdom — I want you to chase wisdom with a pounding heart and reckless abandon. Because, if you fall in love with wisdom you will be richly rewarded.

Wisdom Defined
The Hebrew word for wisdom is *chokmah*. In its simplest form it means skill. For Solomon however, wisdom was much more

than mere skill: it was having the skill appropriate for the situation at hand, in order to produce the best result, according to Kenneth Aitken. Chaim Potok, in his book *Wanderings*, describes wisdom as "the calculated, mannered use of one's skills in the attainment of success."

Wisdom has many sides. For instance:
- Wisdom is technical skill and dexterity.
- Wisdom is intellectual acumen.
- Wisdom means possessing an encyclopedic knowledge of something.
- Wisdom is moral discernment.
- Wisdom is being reverently connected to the source of all wisdom — God.

My own definition of wisdom follows:

Wisdom is highly developed skill and insight applied at the right time to produce the right results for all the right reasons.

Let's break this definition down.

Highly developed skill. Skill is mastery. Skill is the ability to do something well, with proficiency. The person pursuing wisdom seeks a high level of competence and mastery in every aspect of their lives. As they live out their grand purpose they do so with the highest level of skill they can attain.

Insight. Insight is the capacity to discern the true nature of a situation. Insight is that rare ability to see things as they really are — it's gut instinct, a sense of knowing. The person who commits to the Wisdom Lifestyle is also in pursuit of insight. Wisdom is not only about having knowledge and skill, it is also about having an ability to know what's really going on.

Application. It's great to have profound skill. It's very powerful to have insight and discernment, but if you do not apply your skill and insight, it is of no practical value. Knowledge, skill and insight are not the sole ingredients in the alchemy of wisdom. Wisdom must be applied, it has to be used, action has to be taken. If you know what to do but never do it, then it wasn't worth knowing.

Timing. That old Kenny Rogers song is right: "You gotta know when to hold 'em, know when to fold 'em." Applying the knowledge, skill and insight you have developed has to be timed properly. There are times when you should speak and times when you should just shut up; there are times when you should act boldly and times when you should proceed with great caution. Having a divine sense of timing is important if you are to know the power of the Wisdom Lifestyle.

Results. The Wisdom Lifestyle is a lifestyle that focuses on results — right results. You may be the best brick mason in town, but if a carpenter is needed, you cannot deliver the necessary result. Wisdom is about applying the skill, knowledge and insight that you've accumulated to produce the right result.

Motives. Wisdom always has proper motivations at her core. Use wisdom for the right reason. Pride is not the reason to flex wisdom; instead, use wisdom to create positive value in your world and in the lives of the people you touch. The pursuit of wisdom begins with how you think. Wisdom has to become part and parcel of who you are, what you do, and how you live. Wisdom has to be a foundational element of who you are. It has to be the fragrance of your existence. In this chapter I'm asking you to erect this mental pillar: I am asking you to make a commitment, here and now, to fall in love with wisdom; to dig the footings and lay the foundation for the Wisdom Lifestyle. Say to yourself right now:

**From this moment forward
I will pursue wisdom
in all that I am and all that I do.**

Why Love?

Let's talk for a minute about falling in love with wisdom. In order to grow in wisdom, wisdom has to be a priority in your life. One of the easiest ways to fix priorities is through love. Love brings focus, realigns priorities, demands complete attention and has a filtering effect on our lives. Think about it. When you're in love, your thoughts become focused on the object of your love. The lesser things in life fall away as you pursue your beloved with every ounce of your energy and enthusiasm. If you behold the loveliness of wisdom, if you are enamored of wisdom, if you are overwhelmed by wisdom, then your focus will change. Things standing in the way of wisdom will be eliminated. When you're **not** in love, realigning priorities can be difficult, but when you **are** in love, your world is mysteriously reorganized, with the object of your love at the center, and the unimportant things done away with. That's the power of love!

Pursuing wisdom is difficult because it demands *change*. Change is hard. But if you're in love change is easier. If you love wisdom then the change wisdom demands is not as tough. Love takes the sting out of change.

So how does one fall in love with wisdom? Here are three ways:

1. **Allow yourself to be smitten by the beauty of wisdom.** When you see highly developed skill in anything, study it, take it in, learn from it, be inspired by it. I've mentioned Michael Jordan before as a person who exemplifies skill in practice. Watching his skill inspires me to want to develop my own skills more fully. Seeing his excellence in action makes me love excellence and wisdom that much more.

2. **Be vulnerable to wisdom**. Leave yourself open to growth. Always look to learn new things and be open to improving everything about yourself and the way you live your life.

3. **Make a commitment to wisdom**. Decide here and now that your life will be about excellence; that in everything you do you will give your all; that in everything you commit to you will seek to develop the highest level of skill that is attainable, and that you will not only acquire that skill but will also learn how to apply it to the highest good.

How Wisdom Responds to Love

Proverbs chapter three talks about how wisdom responds to love and what it promises to do for you. Those who love wisdom are rewarded with the following: **happiness, long**

life, riches, honor and peace. Now if having all of those things in your life doesn't help you, then you, my friend, are beyond help. But if you are one of those people who long to find these things, then you're gonna love wisdom. Let's take a closer look.

> **Happiness**. Happiness is defined as a "sense of satis-faction." We all want it, but millions of people struggle through each day and wrestle through each night void of any hint of satisfaction.

> Advertisers know of our hunger for happiness — in fact, they count on it. They convince us that we'd be happier if we use [insert product name here]. From cola to clothing, from dream vacations to diet plans, the marketing is directed at our constant craving for happiness. But happiness is internal — a sense of satisfaction or well being. The things that we're of-fered through advertising are, for the most part, ex-ternal, and external remedies don't satisfy internal needs. Wisdom is a much more durable source of happiness. Its magic comes from the fact that it works from the inside out. But how does wisdom work its magic in happiness?

> First, we're happiest when we're learning and grow-ing. Mihaly Csikszentmihalyi says in his book, *Flow*, that we find the magic of optimal experience when we are challenged, when we have to use all of our abilities, when we are stretched in the direction of our potential and purpose.

Wisdom works its internal magic because in order to embrace the Wisdom Lifestyle you have to commit to a life of continual learning and growth, and moreover, to love the process of learning and growing! Think of children when, as toddlers, they are exploring their world. The wonder and joy in their eyes as they take their first steps, speak their first words, ride that bike without training wheels — they're full of life and happiness because every day of their young lives they are learning and growing.

There is a wonderful sense of satisfaction that comes from seeing and sensing growth in your life. Wisdom produces a sense of satisfaction because it causes us to build new levels of competence and to develop a command of those skills which is very satisfying.

Long Life. Long life is also a promise of the Wisdom Lifestyle. People today are very concerned about mortality. Each year billions of dollars are spent trying to stop the aging process. Yet these same people keep habits that shorten and complicate their lives, thus advancing the aging process they so long to stop.

As we pursue wisdom we're called away from life-limiting and life-threatening situations. Those who pursue the Wisdom Lifestyle are drawn to excellence of mind, body and spirit. They pursue the things that enhance their lives, so they live longer. The person living the Wisdom Lifestyle is admonished to depart from evil. Moving away from evil things in our lives reduces stress and thereby extends life.

Riches. Along with long life, the Wisdom Lifestyle brings wealth — not only material wealth, but more importantly, *wealth of spirit.* The reason a person living the Wisdom Lifestyle becomes a magnet for wealth is simple: As you pursue a highly developed skill and insight in your career and learn to apply that skill with impeccable timing, producing profound results for all the right reasons, you will be in great demand! Ask Michael Jordan. When you're in demand you get paid. To paraphrase a line from the movie *Jerry McGuire,* "they show you the money." I refer again to Jordan because he is an excellent example of applied skill and insight. His ability to apply his skill in basketball has made him a magnet for wealth. The same can be said for Pat Summitt, head coach for the University of Tennessee women's basketball program, who has won six national championships. She is highly skilled and insightful as a coach. She gets results. Plus she makes a pretty penny!

Honor. Hand in hand with the wealth-generating power of the Wisdom Lifestyle is wisdom's power to produce honor. If you have developed incredible skill that is being applied with impeccable timing to produce the right results for all the right reasons, it follows that you will be honored and respected.

For example, Mother Theresa had incredible skill for leading young women and for caring for those whom everyone else had given up. We could not help but honor her because of the value she created in this world. And the same can be said for the business manager who finds a way to turn a failing company around by virtue of his skill. Think of all of the honors bestowed on Lee Iacocca for the dramatic turnaround of Chrysler; he was honored because he got the job done. Since we honor people who create value in our world, those who pursue wisdom are honored for that.

Peace.

Honor is fine, but peace is divine.

I was reading an article in *People* magazine recently about Mariah Carey who lives the luxurious life of a pop diva. But one quote from the article haunted me. Mariah Carey said, "I love what I do, but I don't have any peace."

Peace is also an outgrowth of the Wisdom Lifestyle. We all need that sense of calm and certainty that comes from living with a larger purpose, and living full out. Giving yourself totally to each day and finding a way to be a blessing to others with the skills and gifts you've been given and have developed brings peace. The Wisdom Lifestyle produces peace because we remove the cognitive dissonance that comes from knowing that we aren't living up to our potential. It produces peace because the journey is more important than the things we accumulate along the way. Wisdom also moves us away from two things that inevitably rob us of peace — fools and foolishness. As a result, the conflict that comes from relationships with those kinds of people and situations is removed, making way for peace.

The second pillar of wisdom is a call to fall in love with wisdom. **Wisdom is highly developed skill and insight applied at the right time to produce the right results for all the right reasons.** Fall in love with that concept and you will be transformed. No doubt about it! Loving wisdom is really about raising your standards. It's saying to yourself that you will be committed to developing the highest level of skill possible in every area of your life and applying that skill and insight to make your world better.

My life has been radically transformed since I fell in love with wisdom. It is fuller, richer, so much more exciting. Wisdom makes me grow. As I grow in the important areas of my life (as a husband, father, broadcaster, writer, singer, songwriter, producer) I am able to create more value in the world. I am able to be more of a blessing. I love wisdom because it brings out the best in me. It squeezes excellence out of me like a wine press squeezes wine from grapes.

Wisdom will do the same for you, if you LOVE wisdom!

The hand of the diligent shall bear rule: but the slothful will be under tribute.

Proverbs 12:25

Pillar 3

Joyfully Submit To Discipline

Submit to discipline and diligence. Discipline is the mother of skill. Give yourself joyfully to the disciplines that produce the skill and the wisdom you desire. How would your life change if you were more disciplined?

Discipline

The next pillar of the Wisdom Lifestyle is **discipline**. This is where we supercharge our personal effectiveness and chart a course for sustained greatness.

Webster's defines discipline as training that corrects, molds or perfects; to train or develop by instruction; to bring under control; to impose order upon.

Discipline has to be a core value that we live by. We have to make the commitment to joyfully submit to discipline. In every area of our lives in which we desire wisdom, we will have to run the trail of discipline. There are certain habits, skills and disciplines that we must master to be a great father or mother, a great athlete, a great chemist or musician. There are no short cuts.

Herbert Simon, an award-winning philosopher and economist at Carnegie Mellon University, has been studying what makes smart people so smart and what makes highly effective people so effective. This has been his passion for 40-plus years. He says that it all comes down to pattern recognition. He says that really smart and effective people (wise people if you will) have more patterns stored in their brains that they can reference in relation to what they're doing. The great chess player has so many patterns stored up that he can see 20-30 moves ahead.

The great athletes are the same. Take Jordan for example. He says he's seen so many defenses, he's played against so many players trying to shut him down, that when they come at him, he knows what to do to counter their moves and has such a command of skills that he can make his body do what his mind wants to do with great ease.

Herbert Simon says, "It takes at least ten years of hard work — say, 40 hours a week for 50 weeks a year — to begin to do world-class work. We found it takes eight seconds to learn a pattern for a day, and quite a lot longer to learn it permanently." That is discipline. You have to develop patterns and practice them if you are to have mastery of the core skills of whatever you do so you can call those skills up at will. That's wisdom. If you want to be a person full of wisdom, you will have to work.

Discipline Creates Skill
One of the reasons I admire great athletes so much is that their efforts are constantly measured, and they are focused on results. They have to find a way to create value on their team to help them win the game. San Francisco 49ers wide receiver Jerry Rice is one of my all-time favorite athletes because Jerry has learned to love discipline. He doesn't always love the pain involved but he loves the payoff. He gives his best on the playing field and on the practice field, he never slacks and he's intensely focused on being in top form every moment of every day of his life.

Jerry reveals in his autobiography that he practices 150 days in the off-season, seven hours a day. No wonder he doesn't run out of gas in the fourth quarter! No wonder even the rookies in the league have a hard time keeping up with the "old man!" No wonder he has so much "wisdom" as a wide receiver: The skill was birthed from the womb of discipline. He joyfully submits to discipline because the discipline produces skill.

Radio legend Paul Harvey has the same kind of discipline. Twenty-two million people listen to him every day on over 1200 radio stations. They listen to hear him paint pictures of the world we live in and tell us like an old faithful friend what's going on. And he's good. Really good. But he is not good by accident. Even after 66 years in the business, he still gives his all every day. He still goes in before dawn to make sure his broadcast is the best it can be. His discipline gives him the ability to deliver powerful results. There is no doubt about it. The gateway to wisdom (skill and insight) is discipline.

Diligence

Married to the concept of discipline is diligence, which is the consistent application of discipline. To illustrate, I have a friend, J.D. Blair, who's a drummer. I watched for years as he toiled in anonymity. He was a good drummer lost in a world of good drummers. One of my favorite proverbs is the one that says, "The hand of the diligent shall rule." (Proverbs 12:24) J.D. is extremely diligent. He worked on his technique and his skills day after day. He put in hours of work and effort. And in 1998-99, he toured with Shania Twain, one of the biggest tours of the year. His diligence has been rewarded.

To build power in your life, decide to be a person of great discipline and diligence. Finish what you start. Stick with your plan. Develop a level of mastery and apply it consistently. As you become more disciplined and diligent, it is imperative to focus on results. Be sure to develop the right skills, because working hard on the wrong thing is worse than not working at all. For instance, David Letterman had a feature called "Stupid Human Tricks" on his late-night show. I was amazed at the totally useless skills these people had — everything from balancing things on their chins to making perfect replications of animal sounds. All these acts were trotted out for the world to see and for Dave to laugh at. These people had spent years developing skills that had no importance other than being a great joke segment for a late-night TV show. Your discipline should be creating skills that will make you more powerful in the world.

For me, it has boiled down to taking a long hard look at the skills I need to be a man of excellence. In taking a look at my own life, the first thing I had to do was look at my roles and determine the outcomes I wanted to produce, then begin to develop the skills that would take me there, which meant seeking and submitting to the disciplines associated with those skills. After listing my roles and responsibilities, I had to ask myself a very simple yet probing question:

What are the core skills and competencies needed to be highly effective in each of these roles? Am I spending my time developing the skills needed to be effective in these areas?

Tough questions, but they do help clarify why you may feel from time to time that your life isn't going the way you want it to, that somehow you're not living up to your potential. If you haven't taken the time to figure out what you want to contribute to this world, how can you ever open yourself to the opportunities to grow in the direction of your destiny? Do the same for yourself. Make your list. If you find that your heart isn't in it, then break the list and make the one God intended for you to make. Listen to your heart, then order your life so that you will create, through disciplined consistent action, the wisdom needed in that area of your life.

Discipline and diligence not only help you create skill, they help you maintain skill. Look at the order of the natural world. Look at the disciplined, diligent systems operating in your own body. They perform their functions with meticulous precision. Diligence and discipline should be combined with **goals.**

Work to develop a high level of skill and mastery that you can deliver on command. It's one thing to have a skill and quite another to be able to access that skill whenever you need it. Deliver consistently high-quality results like Jerry Rice and Paul Harvey. That means you work to create cycles and systems to ensure that you can deliver quality results on demand.

So how do we put this to work?

By joyfully embracing discipline. Learn to love the disciplines associated with becoming a master of the skill you're pursuing. At all times remember that discipline is the gateway to skill.

Secondly, live a disciplined and well-ordered lifestyle. Look at major areas in your life and expand the goals, or systems and cycles, that help develop high levels of skill and insight. Put in place the kinds of disciplines that will help deliver consistently great results.

- The first is basic to life — a set of disciplines for taking care of yourself. To be clean and healthy, we must master the science of taking care of ourselves. That means disciplined patterns of rest, nutrition, exercise and personal hygiene.

- Second, a set of disciplines and systems is necessary to deliver incredible results in our families and lives of faith.

- Third, a set of disciplines and systems will help make a powerful contribution in our careers.

- Fourth, a set of disciplines and systems will help master our money and resources.

Discipline is the gateway to skill. Diligence is the consistent application of discipline. Joyfully embrace this concept. Live it, and see quantum leaps in your personal levels of positive growth and change in every area of your life.

He that walketh with wise men shall be wise: but a companion of fools shall be destroyed.

Proverbs 13:20

Pillar 4

Walk
With the Wise

Walk with the wise. Choose excellent personal relationships. Make certain that the people closest to you are full of Godly wisdom. Are you growing in your relationships?

They were different. Focused. They wanted to achieve — never wanted to settle for second best. Their drive and enthusiasm was inspiring. They had lots of fun, but when it was time to get down to business, they did. They were a group of outstanding young men that I attended boarding academy with in the little north Georgia town of Calhoun.

Up until I arrived there, I had been a decent student with a GPA of 3.33. Like most teenagers, that was good enough for me, maintaining my academic credibility with my parents and teachers. I didn't take my studies seriously. I wanted to have fun. But things were different in Georgia.

One evening about 9:00, I wandered the halls, looking for a baccarat partner. I stuck my head into Eric Moore's room, chatting excitedly about a game. The room was spotless. Eric, a thoughtful and studious senior, was at his desk studying, as was his friend, Ivan. Their mood was wet with purpose, because the fire of conversation never caught.

When Eric turned to me and said, "Hey man, we're trying to study. We don't have time to play," I was crushed, but dared not show it. As I retreated back down the hallway, his words echoed in my mind. The actions of Eric and Ivan challenged my loose, undisciplined notions about education. I noticed that all the dorm rooms were quiet and clean, that all of the guys were getting down to the business of academic excellence. To fit in here, I was going to have to put the games aside and get to work.

I am so grateful for the influence of those young men. Walking with them caused me to grow. Their friendship and hunger for personal and academic excellence reshaped my life. I have learned as a lover of wisdom that if you are to grow in wisdom you have to make excellent choices in your friendships. The people who speak to the most intimate part of your being are normally the people you admire, and many times they are your friends. People who have your ear, who hold your complete attention, shape who you are, and either draw out of you your true greatness — or bury it. If you want to be a person full of wisdom, you have to embrace this pillar of thought: Walk with the wise.

Many people are dying because of the toxic people they are caught up in close friendships with who smother their light. The Wisdom Lifestyle calls you to be far more selective when it comes to choosing friends and mentors, because these people affect the way you think. And anyone who affects the way you think will ultimately affect the way you live. If you want the full benefit of the Wisdom Lifestyle, you must make up your mind to walk with the wise.

Walking with Wisdom

If you think back to the people who have had the greatest positive impact on your life, you'll find a gallery of folks who caused you to grow. Positive growth is one of the ways you know you're walking with a wise person. The effects of walking with a wise person are profound. Take for example Warren Buffet, one of the richest and most powerful men in the world. He gave some advice to an auditorium filled with students from the University of Washington's business school. He told them to:

"Pick out the person in the class that you admire the most and write down a list of their qualities, then put down the one that, frankly, you could stand the least, and put down the qualities that turn you off. The qualities of the first one you admire are qualities that you, with a little practice, can make your own, and which, if practiced, will be habit forming. I suggest you look at the habits you admire in others, or the behaviors you admire in others, and make those your own habits. And you look at what you really find somewhat reprehensible in others and just decide those are the things you are not going to do."

Buffet said that the problem is that most people get in their own way by installing habits that bind them like chains, quoting Samuel Johnson when he noted, "The chains of habits are too light to be felt until they are too heavy to be broken."

It is interesting to note that Buffet had the good fortune of having great mentors/heroes, and as he continues to succeed he is still growing because of the caliber of people he's chosen to surround himself with. He has benefited from walking with the wise.

Wise Companion/Mentors
So what are the marks of a wise companion mentor? Wise companions, friends or mentors are grounded, growing and glowing.

♦ Grounded

The first test of the wise companion/mentor is that they walk in the fear of God. They are spiritually grounded and have a great deal of respect for the awesome power and wisdom of God. Wise people tend to be doers. Other evidence of their "groundedness" is that they strive to remain free of pride and arrogance. Look for those who are down-to-earth, have a strong sense of the greatness of God, and a simple comfort with who they are. Look for those who are full of personal integrity, who value and demonstrate honesty, trustworthiness, fairness, loyalty, caring and citizenship. Grounded people live by a very high moral code without being self-righteous. They live by the golden rule and treat people like they want to be treated.

♦ Growing

The second test of the great companion/mentor is that they are growing. There is something about people who have committed themselves to excellence: they love to learn and grow. They want to be the best that they can be. They long for skill and insight so that they can make a contribution. Take charge of this aspect of your life. Walk with people who are growing in the important areas of their lives. Walking with people who are growing will inspire you to grow. Go with those who grow!

♦ Glowing

The final test of the wise companion/mentor is that they glow. They glow with a light that emanates from their excellence and their enthusiasm. There is something positively contagious about being around someone who is excellent in what they do and enthusiastic about it. Their energy feeds you.

Donald Davis is the dean of American storytellers. At the annual storytelling festival in Jonesboro, Tennessee, he holds forth with Elvisian grandeur.

I met Donald a couple of years ago and have never been the same since. Here is a man who has mastered his craft, who is full of storytelling wisdom. I've watched him captivate an audience filled with folks from six to sixty-six. They hung on his every word. He is a virtuoso of storytelling. But even before I saw him spellbind a room, I talked with him at length about his craft. As we talked, his eyes danced and sparkled with enthusiasm as he spoke of his life's mission, storytelling. He glowed. After the day I spent with him, I was in love with the art of storytelling. I was changed.

Those who have given themselves to the pursuit of wisdom glow. They shine. It's the birthmark of wisdom.

As you select the ones who will have access to the most intimate places in your heart, the ones you will walk with, choose the ones that glow in humble awe of God, seeking to grow, enthusiastically immersing themselves in excellence.

What About You?

The test of great companion/mentors also applies to you. At some point, somebody will choose you to fill that same role. Live by those virtues you are seeking in others. Be a catalyst for growth in the lives of the people who have chosen you as their companion/mentor.

Building Your Wisdom Circle

As you dive into the Wisdom Lifestyle, it is critical that you surround yourself with companion/mentors in specific areas of your life to help you build wisdom. The following are suggested companion/mentors with whom to seek strong relationships.

The Spiritual Mentor. There is nothing like having someone in your life who has a wonderful relationship with God — someone who is spiritually grounded. For me, my brother Franklin has served in that capacity for many years. He's someone who has committed his life to Christ and is constantly growing in spiritual wisdom. He has taught me about God and helped me to know God: He has caused me to grow. Find someone who will help you grow spiritually. That is a vital relationship.

The Relationship Mentor. If you see people who are prospering in their important relationships, learn as much as you can about what contributes to their success. These are people who have successful relationships with the most important people in their lives. Observe the patterns and habits that lead to the success of their relationships. Ideally, you will want to be in a mentoring relationship where you can ask questions and get feedback as you seek to improve your own relationships.

The Career Mentor. One of the smartest moves you can make is to identify a person who is succeeding in the career field that you are also pursuing and model their habits. Look for balance. Find someone with character and integrity as well as success in their career.

Scott Slade is the morning guy on Atlanta's No. 1-rated news/talk radio station, WSB. I had the pleasure of visiting with him and getting his advice on my own radio career. He has now become one of my broadcasting heroes, and I am a student of his work and a modeler of his work ethic.

Another career mentor is my friend Mr. Hundley Batts, Sr. He is a successful entrepreneur who has taken the time to walk with me as a business mentor.

The Financial Mentor
This is an important one. In the next chapter we'll spend more time talking about money, but for now, I can't stress enough how important it is for you to be in a relationship with someone who has a great deal of financial wisdom.

My brother, Roland, is one of the people in my life who has been a financial mentor. He taught me the true value of a debt-free lifestyle and the wisdom of living within your means. Dave Ramsey, the author and radio show commentator, is another. His books, *Financial Peace*, and *More Than Enough*, have cleared the path for me to achieve financial success.

Having a financial hero in your life is important. Develop a high level of skill and insight in managing and using your money for total effectiveness in life.

The Health and Fitness Mentor
Your health and fitness are important to your ability to make a profound contribution in the world. To that end, you must grow in skill and insight in this area of your life if you are to truly enjoy the benefits of the Wisdom Lifestyle.

It amazes me how neglectful we are of our health and fitness when we are so dependent on it to succeed in life. Have a person in your life that helps you grow in this vital area. Choose a healthy person who can teach you how to eat and exercise properly. You will need energy to live the Wisdom Lifestyle.

The Leadership Mentor
You should have a relationship with someone who knows what it means to lead. As you mature in the Wisdom Lifestyle, you will be marked for leadership. It is important that you learn what it means to be a great leader. Look at the character traits of the leaders that have inspired you, write them down, then model them. In the same way, write down the habits of poor leaders and vow never to have them present in your leadership style.

The People You Shouldn't Walk With
This chapter has been about choices, making the right choices about the people who will walk with you on your journey. We've talked about the importance of choosing to walk with the wise, but another important decision is who **not** to walk with. The wisdom teachers in Solomon's day repeatedly warned against companionship with fools. The same is true today. Many people, young and old, have had their lives destroyed, their potential denied, all because they chose the companionship of fools. If you walk with fools, you will suffer harm. It's as simple as that. The people you walk with shape your life and shape your destiny.

What is a Fool?

According to the dictionary, a fool is one who is deficient in judgment, sense, or understanding. [2] Fools identify themselves in a couple of important ways. One, they show an incredible unwillingness to learn, and two, they lack self-control.

Companionship with fools doesn't work for those pursuing wisdom because fools hate wisdom. They hate to learn. Learning and growth are core values for people pursuing wisdom. If the people with whom you associate hate your core values how can the relationship work? To have a close relationship with a fool is to put yourself in a position where your growth will be stifled.

Lack of self-control is another reason that fools have no place in your inner circle. Through their lack of self-control you will be drawn into situations that will ultimately harm you and cause you pain. And the greatest danger of all is that you may begin to adopt some of their habits and bear the fruits of those habits.

Red Flags of Foolishness

Fools betray themselves by their actions, by speech and conduct. Look at some of the ways that fools identify themselves:

- **Anger**. Fools are given to outbursts of anger. Many express their anger violently or verbally. This anger leads them to act foolishly, and as a result, time

---

[2] ìThe American HeritageÆ Concise Dictionary,î *MicrosoftÆ EncartaÆ 97 Encyclopedia*. The American HeritageÆ Concise Dictionary, Third Edition Copyright ©1994 by Houghton Mifflin Company. Electronic version licensed from and portions copyright ©1994 by INSO Corporation. All rights reserved.

and energy are consumed in dealing with the fallout created by anger. If you give angry people access to influence in your life, you are bound to share in the consequences of their anger. Stay away from fools!

- **Laziness**. Fools are often lazy; they have no direction; they are not doers. Often they choose the path of least resistance, and they hate to work for anything. They wait for a better time or better circumstances and only do what it takes to get by. Proverbs says they turn on their beds like hinges. Lazy people see life through lazy eyes — eyes that are often blinded to opportunity. Therefore, they miss opportunities and don't make a profound contribution to their world. Lazy people should not be part of your circle of companion/mentors. Laziness and wisdom don't mix.

- **Mischief**. Fools look for trouble. They seek out mischief. They're forever in pursuit of it. If they can't find trouble, they make it. I have associated with troublemakers and mischief-seekers a time or two, and every time I have ended up in their net of consequence. Look out for others who are constantly getting into mischief — association with them means sharing in the consequences of their actions. The Wisdom Lifestyle demands better.

- **Scoffing**. Fools are perpetually critical, not acknowledging any views but their own. To be around a person who is constantly critical and negative is draining. There are coaches that stay on the backs of their players, critiquing and evaluating their performance, but at least that has a point. The coach is trying to better his player. The scoffer is negative and critical to no good end. Don't let them gain access to your life.

- **Lying and Gossip**. Fools lie and gossip. There is nothing worse than being in a relationship with someone who lies to you. You cannot have confidence in them, and ultimately their lying will undo the friendship. Truth is essential to companionship in the Wisdom Lifestyle. If you build close relationships with people who lie, you will be lied to. And you will be lied about. Liars lie. You will not be excused from their evil habits.

  Gossip wreaks havoc too. There is a proverb that states, "A tale bearer revealeth secrets." In the essential relationships of your life, the ones that feed you spiritually and that motivate you to live your purpose, you need people that will be true to you, that will keep your confidences. You are not immune to gossip just because you associate with the gossiper.

- **Seducers**. Fools engage in and seek to seduce others to engage in inappropriate sexual relationships. Proverbs has a lot to say about loose women that seduce young men, but now we live in a different age and it applies both ways. Women and men who invite you into inappropriate sexual relationships pave the way for your destruction. Greater than the damage of doing the wrong thing is the danger of becoming the wrong kind of person. Because sex is powerful, it opens us up like nothing else and places us in the position of being easily influenced. When people engage in adulterous activities, they are changed. They become liars. Lying works in direct opposition to wisdom and is time- and energy-consuming. There is the constant worry of fallout from lying. And sooner or later the lies that form the framework of deception will bind like chains. You will suffer in the internal prison of consequence whose bars are not made of what you've done, but rather what you've become. Stay away from those who would lead you into inappropriate sexual relationships. That is foolish behavior.

Fools are an albatross. They are a weight. Fools will bring you harm. Bank on it! As you select the people who will be closest to you on your journey make sure that you keep the wise people in and the fools out.

A core value in the Wisdom Lifestyle is walking with the wise and avoiding the companionship of fools. That concept has to be a bedrock of your thinking. If you will order you life accordingly, you will grow and cause those around you to grow. You will have a greater sense of happiness and fulfillment and will not have to endure the stress that inevitably comes from intimate relationships with foolish people.

Your friends and mentors will help you grow in wisdom. But, the wise person must also handle their money right. In the next chapter we talk about money.

*Be thou diligent to know
the state of thy flocks, and
look well to thy herds.*

Proverbs 27:23

Pillar 5

Master
Your Money

Be a good steward. Master money management. Keep your finances in order. How much better would your life be if your finances were in order?

The Importance of Money

Ever notice how peacefully confident people are when they have their financial house in order? Ever notice how good you feel when all the bills are paid and you have a little bit of extra money? It's a great feeling, isn't it? Wouldn't it be great to feel that way all the time?

I've had the opportunity to meet a number of wealthy people. Many of them do not have the noticeable trappings of wealth — huge house, fancy cars, lots of gold and diamonds. They do, however, possess a great deal of wisdom or skill about money, and they possess a certain amount of (to borrow a phrase from my friend, the great author Dave Ramsey) **financial peace**. I've also had the opportunity to meet a number of people who are struggling financially. Many of them have the trappings of wealth but they haven't trapped any wealth. Often they do not have any skill or wisdom about money.

Money is powerful. It is a wonderful tool. In this modern economy, our system of exchange allows us to provide for the essential things we need and want in life. It builds hospitals and churches and highways, and funds government services. But having money without the knowledge of how to manage and master it is just like having a brand new Ferrari and no keys. Or crazier still, owning the Ferrari and, instead of driving it, pushing it everywhere you want to go.

Mastering your money is a requirement of the Wisdom Lifestyle. Money is a vital tool to be used in living out your destiny in today's times. And to the extent that you sharpen your financial intelligence and your abilities to act on that wisdom, you will prosper beyond your wildest dreams.

Seeking Mastery

One of the main reasons the person living the Wisdom Lifestyle needs to master the stewardship of his money is because he will have an abundance of it. The person full of highly developed skill and insight is a magnet for wealth. People will need your expertise and experience, and if you're the best of the best, you'll be compensated well for it.

There are many people who make a lot of money yet have no wealth. There's a big difference in making money and keeping money, and a big difference in mastering your money rather than having your money master you. That's why one of your companion/mentors should be someone that is a good role model of financial wisdom. Seek to master the basics of handling your resources so that you can use them in the most efficient manner possible to take care of your needs and wants and to be a blessing to your community and your world.

Mastery is about honing the basic skills of money management and discipline so that they are fundamental to the way you think and automatic to the way you act.

Ten Basic Rules of Personal Finance

As I have had the opportunity to talk and walk with people who possess a great deal of financial wisdom, I have grown.

The influences of my brother, Dr. Roland J. Hill, (author of the books *Theoeconomics* and *How to Get Out of Debt)*, and Dave Ramsey (author of *Financial Peace* and *More Than Enough*) have helped shape my thinking about money. In reading and researching the writings in Proverbs, there are also some key themes that emerge over and over. After years of interviewing some of the richest people in America on my daily radio talk show and reading hundreds of books on the subject, I have developed ten basic rules of personal finance that are ratified in the wisdom teachings of Proverbs.

1. **Spend Less Than You Earn.** One thing that I've learned from the proverbs and from great financial writers and teachers is that you shouldn't spend what you don't have. Order your life so that you can live within your means. It doesn't matter how much you make. The man who makes $200,000 a year and spends $210,000 is no better off than the man who makes $20 and spends $22. Both end up with a negative net worth.

   The financially savvy people that I've met find a way to live on much less than they make. Sir John Templeton, one of my financial heroes, sought to live his life on 50 percent of his income. Living the Wisdom Lifestyle means finding a way to live below your means and creating a buffer of abundance. You should have more than you need, and if you have more than you need, you can help others and you can build a foundation for your family's future that will last throughout generations.

2. **Tithe.** Part of reverencing God is knowing that all you have and own belongs to Him. Make it a basic part of your financial plan to joyfully return to God ten percent of all you earn. I have read story after story about the people who are faithful in paying their tithe being blessed over and over. There is a biblical promise that if you tithe, you will be blessed. But I see something more practical in the paying of tithes.

    First, trusting God with your money is an incredible act of faith. It's a tangible way of fearing God. Second, it gets you into the habit of living below your means since your planning now is built around 90 percent of your income. Third, it gives you practice in financial discipline. You learn how to allocate money in specific areas and have the discipline to be true to that allocation. It primes you to budget the rest of your income.

3. **Pay Yourself First.** After you've paid your tithe, pay yourself. Most financial experts agree that you ought to save and invest ten percent of everything you earn, but I'm a bit more aggressive in my thinking. Save and invest as much as you possibly can: 30-50 percent is a great goal to me. In that way, you'll be keeping what you work so hard to earn.

Another Warren Buffet story serves as a great illustration. It is said that he was playing bridge, and his friends were talking about the huge salaries a number of corporate executives were making. They went on and on about it until finally, in exasperation, Buffet declared, "Don't tell me how much they made! Tell me how much they kept!"

The wealth you generate should be managed in such a way that you keep some of it. Pay yourself. Remember, it's not only how much you make, it's how much you keep.

4. **Live Debt Free.** Be a lender, not a borrower. The borrower is slave to the lender, it's that simple. A debt free lifestyle represents greater freedom.

   How much better would your life be if you didn't owe anybody anything but love? No car note, no house note, no credit cards. It's possible to be debt-free, but it begins with how you think. See yourself as living debt-free and let it become a core operating principle.

   To get there, first lose the credit cards. If you must, keep one for travel and make it American Express so that it is paid off each month. From there, create a list of your debts from smallest to largest, and apply every penny you have to eradicating those bills that are weighing you down and keeping you from building any real wealth. By eliminating debt, you will be better able to invest your income and increase your wealth.

For example, suppose you could invest your monthly car payment and house note. The average house note is $900 per month, and the average car payment is $300 per month, so that would create $1200 per month that you could invest. Invested at a conservative eight percent return, in ten years you will have accumulated over $204,000 and in 30 years you'll have close to 1.8 million.

Keep as much of your money as you can, and save and invest as much of it as you can. Think of how much good you can do with the tool of wealth at your disposal.

5. **Plan for the Big Stuff**. You've got to have a game plan. In everyone's life, there are several major events to plan for. The two biggies are retirement and college education for your kids. I encourage you to find a wise financial planner and get to work planning for these major events right now.

    Many events just seem to slip up on us, but so many more are predictable. You know you'll have to have money when you stop working, and you know your kids will need money to get a great education. If you don't set this money aside, how will you get it?

    I have a young friend who made a plan in his early 20s that would allow him to retire at 45. When I had lunch with him recently, he told me he's way ahead of schedule. His discipline is paying off.

My barber is much the same way. I was there the day he was laid off from his job. He didn't miss a beat. In fact, it didn't seem to bother him. He had saved and prepared, so he was ready when the layoff came. He had a plan.

Start your preparations now. Find a financial advisor you can trust. Get the wisdom you need to make a plan to take care of the big stuff.

6. **Have an Emergency Fund**. Life is full of emergencies. Some of them are predictable: car trouble, sickness, job loss, the need to travel immediately. All of these things seem to happen to us all. So why don't we plan for them?

   It's important that you build up a sizeable emergency fund, about six months to a year's worth of living expenses. I refer again to my barber because he's got a lot of common sense. When he was laid off, he didn't panic because he had a reserve fund. He knew without a doubt that he could make it without the income from his full-time job. If you were called today on the job and told that you were no longer needed, could you make it without the income? The Wisdom Lifestyle calls you to make that kind of financial planning and preparation.

   One additional note: Have an additional fund that you set aside to help others. This will allow you to help your friends and family when they are in need without destroying your personal financial plan.

7. **Live On A Budget**. The word budget triggers thoughts of a life of drudgery without any fun. Not true! A budget simply means that you plan how you will allocate your resources. Every dollar has a destination.

   Life works on systems and cycles. Every bit of food we eat is budgeted by our bodies. The same should be true of our financial world. A budget allows us to command and control our resources and allows us to know with precision what is going out and coming in, and where our money is being spent. That will give us greater power to make better decisions about our futures. Build your financial future by building a budgeting system to help take care of today and tomorrow.

8. **Keep Meticulous Records.** It is important to keep concise and thorough records. File receipts, and keep all insurance policies, tax information, payroll information, wills and other important documents in a safe, convenient location. Part of having financial wisdom is keeping an eye on business. Keeping good records forces us to pay attention.

9. **Set Financial Goals.** One of the best things we can do is to set goals. Setting goals has enriched my life more than I can adequately express. I remember the first time I set financial goals for myself. I was in a bookstore with my dear friend, Shelbert. We found a book that talked about figuring out how much money you need to live your dreams.

We followed the formula outlined in the book and quickly did the calculations in our minds. WOW! When I came to my figure, I was stunned. I had never thought that way before. Everybody at some time says they want to be a millionaire, but how many ever really map it out? I looked at Shelbert. He looked at me. Then we looked around the store as if the thought police were going to come and haul us off to jail for thinking outside of our normal thought patterns.

After we left the store, we both began setting higher financial goals. That was over ten years ago, and I can say that both of our lives have been changed in ways that we never could have imagined. And they never would have changed if we hadn't imagined things differently.

Set your financial goals. Write down how much you need to live the lifestyle you've always dreamed of. Write down what you need for retirement, for the kids' college educations. And make sure you write down how much you want to give away. Part of your long-range plan should include the contributions you want to make. Then build a plan to make it happen.

10. **Read Before You Write.** We wrap this section up with a little old-fashioned common sense. Read things before you sign them! Read things before you sign them! Read things before you sign them!

I can't say that enough. In financial matters, it is of the utmost importance that you understand what you're getting into and know the consequences of your financial commitments. If the people you're dealing with feel uncomfortable with you reading any documents related to a business transaction, cut your ties with them immediately.

- Understand your investments.
- Understand your insurance coverage.
- Understand your estate plan.
- Understand all of your legal arrangements.
- Keep an eye on your business.
- Reading is fundamental.
- Live by that.

By taking control of your finances you position yourself for leadership. I've met many people who have great dreams but are powerless to do anything about their dreams because of financial problems. They can't lead because their financial crises tie them down and zap their confidence.

When you have mastered your money you will feel more empowered to lead. Getting that monkey off your back and putting it back in the cage will free you up to be a leader in your world.

By justice a king gives stability to the land, but one who exacts gifts ruins it.

Proverbs 29:4

Pillar 6

Lead from the Inside Out

Lead from the inside out. Lead those in your sphere of influence by example and service. Develop a reputation for justice, fairness, and honor that is applied without respect of persons. How many people could you positively impact if you were a better leader?

Leading on the Inside

"By justice a king gives stability to the land, but one who exacts gifts ruins it." Proverbs 29:4

To lead is to direct the course of something, to guide behavior or opinion, to direct performance, to act as a commander, director or guide. Growth as a leader begins internally. It begins with the decision to direct the course of your own life and be responsible for where you are, and more importantly, where you are going.

Let me ask you a couple of questions:
- How will you lead your own life if you have not decided on a direction?
- How will you chart your course in life if you don't have a destination in mind?
- How will you know if you are living with power and purpose if you haven't decided what it means to live?

There are scores of people who want to be leaders, yet they have no idea where they're going. Before you can lead in the outside world, you have to take command of your inner world and become a person of great self-control and discipline. This is the greatest work you will ultimately do because it affects everything else in your life. Part of the process of internal leadership has to do with settling on fundamentals.

You have to have a strong set of internal values to guide your life. Establishing a set of internal values that guide you will lift you to heights unimaginable. There are a number of books that will help you in creating a system of core values by which to guide your life. The best I've come across is the *Seven Habits of Highly Effective People,* written by Stephen Covey. The principles expressed in this book are a good set of core values to include in your own list. The *Character Counts* organization holds up six character virtues that serve as great foundations:

- ♦ Caring
- ♦ Citizenship
- ♦ Respect
- ♦ Responsibility
- ♦ Loyalty
- ♦ Trustworthiness

Internal leadership is about knowing who you are. It's about your core values. Make a decision on how you will use your inner strength to make a contribution to your outer world. People need a purpose in life. Mine is to encourage people to live their dreams and to love wisdom.

Once you know who you are and what kind of contribution you'd like to make, it's time to set some specific written goals for your life. Since there are tons of resources out there to help you with goal-setting, I'm not going to spend a lot of time on this topic, other than to say that you need to know what you want to accomplish. **Write it down!** Writing it down gives power to your plan. List the steps involved in the process. Have goals. Internal leadership is about setting the tone and tempo for your life. It's about joyfully taking responsibility for the direction of your life.

Once you have established and settled on your core values, the contribution you'd like to make, and the goals for your life, then the job of internal leadership becomes twofold:

1. To take action.
2. To hold yourself accountable for being true to your core values and your purpose in life.

Internal leadership is about acting on your goals and purpose in life. It is about doing today the things that need to be done in connection with the goals you've set and the daily contributions you long to make to this world. Internal leadership is about being driven by your values, purposes and goals rather than being driven by your feelings. Your power will grow as you learn to keep your word to yourself. Your power will grow as you hold yourself accountable for living by your core values.

Here's the neat thing: As you lead your inner world, you will begin to shine in your outer world. People will see the glow of order in your inner world, and they will want you to help bring that same order to the outer world.

Get yourself together on the inside to be truly effective outside. Do the work. Hunker down and remodel your inner living space. Clean it up. And keep it clean.

Leadership

As you mature along this continuum of excellence called the Wisdom Lifestyle, you'll find that people will want you to lead. You'll find yourself wanting to serve. It's the combination of the two that make for great leadership. Think about it. The man or woman that is right with God, committed to excellence, disciplined, surrounded by excellent companions and mentors, financially secure and stable is in a prime position to make an incredible contribution to the world.

My friend, Jim Haslam II, says that a leader is someone that people will follow. That is so true. But great leaders are also great servants, and great leaders also move people in the right direction.

We live in a time when people don't want to lead. Partly because it's such a hassle and partly because most people are so preoccupied with their own lives that there is little time left to be concerned with the lives of other people. But our world is made so much better by wise leaders. Families are stronger when there is wise leadership. Communities are stronger. States are stronger. Nations are stronger when led by wise men and women. As you become a person of wisdom and excellence, you will find yourself called into the decision-making processes of your community. Your light will attract them.

Leadership is about service. Public leadership, whether in the PTA, in public office, at church, little league, is about taking your set of skills and applying them to create value and growth in service to mankind.

The wisdom schools of King Solomon's time were designed to teach young men how to be leaders. The young men were taught the value of righteousness, fairness and justice.

Righteousness
Great leaders seek to live good lives. They are marked by integrity. They keep their word. We live in a time when people are afraid of this notion. The standard copout is that no one is perfect. That is true, but leaders should feel compelled to be pacesetters of personal integrity, and they should surround themselves with people that also value and honor integrity.

As you are called into positions of leadership, make certain that you act with the utmost respect and integrity in all dealings. As you do, you'll inspire confidence in your leadership and will have a powerful impact on those serving with you.

Fairness
It's disheartening to see someone in leadership who doesn't treat people fairly. On a number of occasions, I have witnessed the unfair way in which people are treated based on their perceived position in society. There have been times when I was treated one way because someone didn't know me, and then quite the opposite ten minutes later by the same organization simply because someone recognized me. Great leaders have it in their hearts to be fair at all times. As a leader you must be fair. You must treat all people with dignity and respect.

Justice

In positions of leadership you'll be called upon to make some tough decisions. You will have to administer justice. Justice will demand of you insight and intelligence. Think about the long-term ramifications of the decisions you make. Think about what is truly best for the people you serve. Think about the precedents you will set as you make decisions. See the big picture. That's where your years of insight and your connection with God pay off, big-time.

Solomon was forced into a position of leadership at the age of 12. His connection with God, coupled with what he experienced as the son of a king, gave him the insight to make good decisions as a leader.

Intelligence. You also need intelligence. You need to know the facts of a given situation, **all** the facts. That's why you, as a leader, have to keep your eyes open and your ears to the ground. Have a council of advisors of the highest caliber whom you can trust implicitly. Learn all you can before making a decision or rendering a judgment. Consult God: He should chair the board.

Decisiveness. Another mark of the great leader is decisiveness. Great leaders make decisions. They move the ball forward. They make the call. The mature leader will be decisive. After weighing all the facts carefully, he or she will make a decision.

Great leaders move. Once a decision has been made, great leaders make things happen. When they make a decision, they follow through, they make sure that plans are implemented. They follow up and they follow through. In order to have that kind of confidence, you have to be sure of who you are and where you stand with God. That confidence is born of fearing God and knowing that you are a person of integrity.

The Wisdom Lifestyle is one of personal and public leadership. As we mature as people of wisdom, we will grow into positions of leadership. It is in those positions that we have the greatest opportunity to infuse our world with the very wisdom that has transformed us.

Great leaders:
- Take care of their people
- Are fair and honest
- Live with integrity
- Surround themselves with the best & brightest
- Think long-term
- See the big picture
- Pay attention
- Are decisive
- Are just
- Make certain that they look to God for direction and light

It is important that you seek wisdom in this area, that you study leadership. One way is to identify great leaders in your world. Ask yourself what are the qualities they possess that make them great leaders and begin to model those qualities.

The righteous considereth the cause of the poor: but the wicked regardeth not to know it.

Proverbs 29:7

Pillar 7

Lend Yourself
To the Poor

Lend yourself to the poor. Give back to those who have less than you. Give them the gift of wisdom. Give them the knowledge that will empower them to rise above their circumstances. Show them your God. How much of a blessing can you be to those in need if you give them the gift of wisdom wrapped in love?

As you grow in wisdom you will be intoxicated by a desire to help others. This is where the Wisdom Lifestyle becomes most powerful, when you reach out and help those less fortunate in your community. Your level of service to your community is not measured in dollars given, but rather in lives changed. Community service shows up in the lives of the people you choose to serve. The best thing you can give someone is wisdom.

I was talking to my barber again and we had an extended conversation about the best way to help people. He reminded me of the old proverb, "If you give a man a fish, he'll eat for a day. If you teach a man to fish, he eats for life." We need more people who serve their communities by helping others find and exploit their potential.

The Service Mindset

People living the Wisdom Lifestyle possess what I call a service mindset. They want very much to help in any way they can. They love making a difference. They love having jumper cables in their cars. They look for opportunities to serve and make the world a better place. The funny thing is that as you give, it is given to you. If you give yourself away to your community, you'll feel great. You get a high from helping others that can't be created by anything else. This is where you put your wisdom to work, because you are finding ways to use your arsenal of skills to create results for all the right reasons.

So how do you serve? First, make an inventory of your greatest skills and look for places to plug them in where they are needed in your community.

Second, become an evangelist for the Wisdom Lifestyle. It's one thing to help out a Big Brother/Big Sister organization; it's quite another to change someone's thinking and thereby change their destiny.

If you love wisdom, then you should love impregnating your world with wisdom.

Conclusion

This book has been a work of love for me. I truly love wisdom. I love what it has the power to do in people's lives. I wrote this book for you. I want more than anything for you to allow these pillars to form the foundation of your thinking. I know that your life will improve in ways you never could have imagined. I want you to see how awesome God is and to walk in fear and reverence of Him. I want you to be on-line with God and to draw from His infinite wisdom and insight. I want you to commit every cell of your body to excellence and wisdom. I want you to pursue skill and insight with every fiber of your being. I want you to value wisdom wherever you see it and hold on to it like your life depends on it, because it does. I want you to joyfully submit to discipline: It is the gateway to skill. As you live a disciplined life, you'll enjoy growth that will empower you to have a profound impact on your world.

I want you to choose wise companions and mentors. The people that are closest to you will help to shape your destiny. Those people should be championship caliber. As you walk with the wise, you'll grow in wisdom.

I want you to live in financial abundance. By mastering the basics of personal finance, you will gain the power to live the life you've always dreamed of. You will also be empowered to help those around you to prosper.

I want you to take your wisdom out into the field and serve as leaders. Looking out for people. Helping them to grow.

Moving your families and communities forward. Helping to fill the organizations in your world with wisdom.

I want you to serve your fellow man. Those less fortunate should benefit from your growth and maturity. Find a way to use your wisdom by serving. Make the circle complete.

The seven pillars of wisdom is a continuum of excellence that connects to create the Wisdom Lifestyle. It begins with changing the way you think. Changing the way you think changes the way you act. Changing the way you act re-shapes your destiny.

Therefore these principles must be memorized, internalized and actualized.

The Memory Plan

The students of the wisdom teachers of Solomon's day were called upon to memorize the proverbs so they would have instant access to profound wisdom as they made decisions in the everyday matters of life. The same is true here. To that end, I want you to memorize the seven proverbs that form the foundations of each chapter. They follow on the next page.

The fear of the Lord is the beginning of wisdom.

Proverbs 1:7

Wisdom is the principal thing; therefore get wisdom: and with all thy getting get understanding.

Proverbs 4:7

The hand of the diligent shall bear rule: but the slothful will be under tribute.

Proverbs 12:25

He that walketh with wise men shall be wise: but a companion of fools shall be destroyed.

Proverbs 13:20

Be thou diligent to know the state of thy flocks, and look well to thy herds.

Proverbs 27:23

By justice a king gives stability to the land, but one who exacts gifts ruins it.

Proverbs 29:4

The righteous considereth the cause of the poor: but the wicked regardeth not to know it.

Proverbs 29:7

About the Author

Hallerin Hilton Hill is a radio talk show host, motivational speaker, trainer and wisdom crusader who lives and works in Knoxville, Tennessee. In addition to his radio work and speaking he is a TV commentator and successful songwriter, having written for Grammy award-winning artists Whitney Houston and Take 6, as well as many others. Hill is a graduate of Oakwood College in Huntsville, Alabama, where he studied Communications. He lives with his wife, Nedra, and their two children, Hallerin II & Halle Nicole. Hill is the CEO and founder of Wisdom House, a multimedia company focused on inspiring people around the world to grow in wisdom.